# Football's RUGGED RUNNING BACKS

The SPORTS HEROES Library

# Football's RUGGED RUNNING BACKS

## Richard Rainbolt

Lerner Publications Company • Minneapolis

ACKNOWLEDGMENTS

The illustrations are reproduced through the courtesy of: p. 6, San Diego Chargers; pp. 8, 57, 67, 70, Vernon J. Biever; pp. 11, 14, 16, 19, 21, 25, 29, 32, 35, 39, 41, 44, 45, 50, 59, 61, 64, Pro Football Hall of Fame; pp. 37, 53, Baltimore Colts; p. 47, New York Football Giants.

Cover photo by Vernon J. Biever

LIBRARY OF CONGRESS CATALOGING IN PUBLICATION DATA

Rainbolt, Richard.
   Football's rugged running backs.

   (The Sports Heroes Library)
   SUMMARY: Brief biographies emphasizing the careers of ten noted running backs: Jim Thorpe, Red Grange, Ernie Nevers, Steve Van Buren, Joe Perry, Ollie Matson, Hugh McElhenny, Lenny Moore, Jim Brown, and Gale Sayers.

   1. Football—Biography—Juvenile literature.   2. Backfield play (Football)—Juvenile literature.   [1. Football—Biography. 2. Backfield play (Football)]   I. Title.

GV939.A1R35        796.33'2'0922[B][920]        74-27469
ISBN 0-8225-1052-9

Published simultaneously in Canada by
J. M. Dent & Sons (Canada) Ltd., Don Mills, Ontario

Manufactured in the United States of America

International Standard Book Number: 0-8225-1052-9
Library of Congress Catalog Card Number: 74-27469

# Contents

Football is one of the most punishing of the contact sports. Each football player takes a great risk every time he steps onto the field. This is especially true of the running back. He receives the greatest recognition of all the players, but he also pays a high price for his fame. A running back, more than any other player, must learn to live with the thought that his career could be ended by injury at almost any time.

If a man is a good running back, the opposing team may change its defense just to stop him. He will be hit many times during a game. Time and again, he will find himself under several hundred pounds of defenders.

During this constant pounding, he may suffer a foot, ankle, or knee injury that keeps him from running his best. He may then find that he is not

Gale Sayers, one of football's great running backs

useful to his team any more. The history of college and professional football is full of stories about great runners cut down by injuries at the high point of their careers. Unlike quarterbacks or linemen, few great runners can take the punishment past their mid-30s. Those who do, as well as those who don't, carry the scars of their trade. Stitches and knee operations are common among running backs.

A few of the great players, like Jim Thorpe, were so strong and in such good condition that they were stopped only by age. And a few have even left the game at the peak of their powers and in good health. Jim Brown was one of the few to do this.

This is a book about some of the greatest running backs ever to play the game. All of these backs played professional ball. All but Jim Thorpe played on college teams as well.

There are many other famous running backs who are not included in this book. This is because not even experts can agree on who the greatest running backs of all time were. To the players in this book could be added Cliff Battles or Johnny Blood. Or Bronko Nagurski, Clarke Hinkle, George McAfee, Charley Trippi, Frank Gifford, Paul Hornung, Jim Taylor, Tommy Mason, Don Perkins, Cookie Gilchrist, Abner Haynes, Mike Garrett, or Alan Ameche. The list is endless.

On the football fields today are other fine running backs. Some experts will say that these players should be named among the best. But only time and luck will be the judges of that.

## Jim Thorpe

No other person in American sports has achieved greater success than the famous Indian athlete Jim Thorpe. There seemed to be no athletic accomplishment beyond his reach. He was not only a great football star, but he was also a big-league baseball player. And in 1912, during the Olympic Games, his display of athletic skills made him a sports hero for the whole world.

Thorpe was born in 1888, in a small farm house in Oklahoma. His mother was mostly Sac and Fox Indian. His father was half Sac and Fox, and half Irish. As a child Jim was given the Indian name *Wa-Tho-Huck*, which means "bright path." It turned out to be a name with meaning. Jim Thorpe was to blaze a bright path across the pages of American sports history.

Young Jim spent his early years on his father's farm in Oklahoma. He developed a strong, swift body as he roamed the fields and woods. At the Indian reservation school he attended, Jim became an outstanding athlete. Then, at the age of 19, he went off to the famous Carlisle Indian School in Pennsylvania, where he joined the football team. The Carlisle team had recently gained national football fame by playing and beating some of the large universities in the East and the Midwest.

Jim did not care much about his studies at Carlisle. And he did not work very hard at football practice. During the team's games, Jim got in very little playing time. He was sent in to play only when someone on the field got hurt. Then his big chance came in a game against a strong, unbeaten Pennsylvania team. The regular halfback was injured, and the coach had to put Thorpe in. That day, Jim Thorpe ran for touchdowns of 85 and 65 yards. Little Carlisle handed Pennsylvania its only defeat of the season.

After spending two years at Carlisle, Jim left the school. He decided that he wanted to travel for a while. So he signed up with a semi-pro base-ball team for $15 a week, and traveled around the country playing baseball. Then in 1911, he re-turned to Carlisle and football. By that time, Jim was a swift and powerful runner and a tremendous kicker. He could drop-kick field goals from the 50-yard line. Jim's skill was rewarded when he was named to both the 1911 and 1912 All-America teams.

Jim Thorpe was becoming known as the greatest football player of his day. But that was only part of his fame. In 1912, after he graduated from Carlisle, Jim went to Sweden to compete in the Olympic Games against the great track and field athletes of Europe. Two of the hardest contests in the competition were the decathlon and the pentathlon. In these contests the athletes had to be good in many different events—long-distance running events and dashes, as well as throwing events. The athletes had to be able to jump high and jump long. They even had to jump over hurdles while they were running. Jim Thorpe could do all of these things well. No one was surprised when he won gold medals in both the decathlon and pentathlon.

*Jim Thorpe punting during a pre-game warm-up*

Later, Thorpe was stripped of his Olympic medals and records. The Olympics were for amateur athletes only, and Jim had played baseball for money before going to Sweden. His gold medals were offered to the runners-up in the pentathlon and decathlon. But they would not take the awards. They knew that the real winner was Jim Thorpe. The medals and trophies were sent to Lucerne, Switzerland, and put in a display case. They are there today.

After the 1912 Olympics, Jim Thorpe played professional baseball for a few seasons. But his real success came when he signed up with the pro football Canton Bulldogs. He received $250 for each game he played—almost three times as much as most other players of that day. Thorpe played with the Bulldogs for several hard-hitting years.

During those early days of pro football, the players did not wear heavy padding as today's players do. Football was a very rough, very dirty game. Often players would try to get another team's star off the field by injuring him. Thorpe, who was over 6 feet tall and weighed 190 pounds, was always the target of opposing tacklers. But this did not bother him. Sometimes he would tell the other team which way he was going to run with the ball. The players who tried to stop him felt

as though they had been hit by a freight train. In spite of the brutal way the game was played, Jim never suffered a serious injury.

Jim Thorpe had a hard life after he quit football in 1929. Because he had not saved much money during his career, he was very poor. To forget his problems, Jim began to drink heavily. Then came the Depression, a time when work was hard to find. During these years, Jim supported himself by working as a common laborer. Later, during World War II, he worked as a carpenter on a ship. In 1953, Jim Thorpe died at the age of 65.

Jim's name does not appear in the football record books because few accurate records were kept in his day. Even if records had been kept, the statistics would have told little of Jim Thorpe's abilities. Jim was outstanding in lacrosse, boxing, basketball, archery, skating, and almost any other sport he tried. He was the greatest all-around athlete this century has seen.

*Jim Thorpe (center) poses with team officials of the Rock Island Independents in 1925.*

## *Red Grange*

On October 18, 1924, the University of Illinois dedicated a new football stadium. On that same day, Harold "Red" Grange gave the most exciting display of running ever seen during football's early years. If Red Grange is remembered for anything he did, it will be for his play against the Michigan Wolverines that day.

Grange was then a junior halfback for Illinois, one of the most powerful teams in the country. Michigan was also an unbeaten national power. The Michigan defense was so strong that it had given up only three touchdowns in 20 games. Playing in earlier games for Illinois, Grange had surprised the football world with his long touchdown runs. But in spite of his skill, no one thought that Illinois could win against the Wolverines.

Before the game, the Michigan coach bragged that there would be 11 Michigan tacklers on top of Grange every time he got the ball. At the start of the game, Michigan dared the redhead to run.

On the kick-off they booted the ball to Grange at the 5-yard line. He ran first to the sidelines, then inside, and then upfield. He danced and dashed through the Michigan defense on his way to a 95-yard touchdown.

This stunned the Michigan fans. But they had only to wait a short time to see the Grange magic again. Michigan punted to the Illinois 33-yard line, and Grange picked it off. He took the ball and started upfield, once again threading his way through the Wolverine tacklers. He ran 67 yards for a touchdown without a Michigan defender touching him.

After the kick-off, Michigan could not move the ball. So they punted, and Red caught it at the Illinois 44. He floated through the Wolverines for *another* touchdown. Minutes later he took the ball on the Michigan 45 and ran for his fourth score. The first half of the game was over.

Against the most powerful defensive team of his time, Grange had run for four long touchdowns in 12 minutes! People who saw the game claimed that no one laid a hand on Red during any of those runs. But the famous Michigan defense was to have even more trouble with Grange. In the second half he threw a touchdown pass. Later, he ran 12 yards for his fifth score of the game.

When the game was over, underdog Illinois had beaten Michigan, 39-14. Grange had carried the ball 21 times for six touchdowns and over 400 yards. Because of the way he had slipped through the Michigan defense, Grange was nicknamed "The Galloping Ghost."

The man who won the game for Illinois that day was born in Pennsylvania in 1903. He later moved with his family to Wheaton, Illinois. When Red was eight years old, a doctor told him that he had a bad heart and should not take part in sports. He tried out for the high school football team anyway.

Red was a skinny kid, weighing only 138 pounds, but he still scored 75 touchdowns in high school play. When he went to the University of Illinois, no one thought that he could make the football team. At 166 pounds, he was just too light. But during summers away from school, he took a job hauling 75-pound blocks of ice. This work made his body much tougher, and it enabled him to make the team. At 6 feet and a strong 170 pounds, Grange could not be stopped. He seemed to run without effort. When tacklers leaped at him, he would turn suddenly and then take off in another direction with instant speed. It was those "ghost-like" runs that brought him national attention. He was named to the All-America team three times, as he led Illinois to victory after victory.

In 1925, after graduating from Illinois, Red went on to play professional football. The pro sport has not been the same since then. Grange signed with the Chicago Bears, and great crowds turned out to see the redhead play. In both New York and Los Angeles, 70,000 fans packed the stadiums to watch Grange and the Bears. After a while, business people named soft drinks, shoes, and sports clothes after him. Red even played parts in two movies. He had become pro football's first big star.

Red's six seasons with the Bears were good ones. But in 1927, a knee injury threatened his career. Though Red's knee healed well and his speed remained good, his running was not the same. "After that injury," he said, "I was just another halfback." But that was not true. Grange was still a good passer, and he could still outrun most of the other players. In 1931, he was named to the first all-star team of the National Football League (NFL). During the next few years, he played in the same backfield with Bronko Nagurski, another famous running back. These two led Chicago to NFL titles and record-breaking rushing totals.

In 1935, Red Grange retired from professional football. Today, the redhead is remembered as one of the fastest and cleverest running backs in football history.

## Ernie Nevers

Ernie Nevers played three professional sports in the 1920s—basketball, baseball, and football. As a big league baseball player, he helped to set one of baseball's lasting records. Ernie's greatest fame, however, came through playing pro football. He holds a scoring record in football that has stood for over 40 years.

Ernie Nevers was born in Willow River, Minnesota, in 1903. A few years later, his family moved to Superior, Wisconsin, where he spent most of his early years. Ernie did not learn to play football until he went to Superior Central High School. He was a good player, but he was better known for his skill in basketball. Under Ernie's leadership, Superior Central won the state baske championship. (Some people say that Ernie ... vented the hook shot during his years as a high school basketball player.)

After high school, Ernie went to California to attend Stanford University. It was there that he

To Olaf Hougvard, to
friend and...
...ever met.
...im

Juniata Valley Elementary School
Alexandria, Penna.

met Pop Warner, one of the greatest college coaches of all time. (Warner had been Jim Thorpe's coach at the Carlisle Indian School.) Under Pop Warner's direction, Ernie worked at developing his own football skills. He started as a halfback on the Stanford team, but Warner soon moved him to fullback. In that position he could take the ball on almost every play. By his third year at Stanford, Ernie had become one of the best all-around college players of his day. He displayed great power in passing, kicking, and running.

In Ernie's last year at Stanford, he broke his ankle and missed all but the last game of the regular season. In that game he injured his other ankle. This was a great blow to his team, because Stanford was to play the Fighting Irish of Notre Dame in the Rose Bowl. And Stanford could not win that game without Ernie Nevers.

Knowing this, the Stanford coaches made a special cast for Ernie's leg. With this cast and a pain-killing shot, Ernie was able to play the whole game against the Fighting Irish. Even with his bad leg, Ernie rushed for 114 yards. But the Irish still won, 27-10.

After graduation, Ernie started his three pro sports careers. He played only a few games of pro basketball. And he played pro baseball for only three seasons. But during one of those seasons he helped to set one of baseball's most famous records. In 1927, the great Babe Ruth stunned the baseball world by hitting 60 home runs. Two of those home-run balls were thrown by a young pitcher for the St. Louis Browns—Ernie Nevers. That was one record-setting event in which Ernie would gladly *not* have taken part.

Ernie's pro football career was more successful than his careers in the other sports. He played only five seasons—two with the Duluth Eskimos and three with the Chicago Cardinals. But even in that short time, he became known for his toughness and his determination.

When Ernie was with the Eskimos, they always played a rugged schedule against the best pro teams. In 1926, the Eskimos played 29 games in 112 days. In all, Ernie missed only 27 minutes of play. (Trouble with his appendix kept him out for almost half of one game!)

That was the way Ernie Nevers was. He shook off pains and injuries that would have kept other men from playing. He stubbornly refused to quit. But that same stubborness drove him to the limits of his ability. He would carry the ball even when the defense was set against him. Ernie just hammered away at the defense until it gave in.

In one game, Nevers completely clobbered the defense. It happened on a very cold Thanksgiving Day in 1929. Ernie Nevers' Chicago Cardinals were playing the Chicago Bears for the city championship. Ernie scored all his team's points as the Cardinals beat the Bears, 40-6. There have been only two men who have come close to this record in 40 years. Dub Jones, in 1951, and Gale Sayers, in 1965, each scored six touchdowns and 36 points.

In 1931, after a tough five years in the National Football League, Ernie Nevers retired. He went back to help Pop Warner coach the Stanford team. Years later, Warner was asked who was the greatest football player that he had ever coached. Many people were sure he would say that it was Jim Thorpe. They were surprised when he claimed that it was Nevers. "Ernie Nevers could do everything that Thorpe could do," he said. "And he always tried harder than Thorpe. Ernie gave 60 minutes of himself in every game. But I seldom got more than 20 out of Thorpe."

*Steve Van Buren*

Steve Van Buren was born in Honduras, Central America, in 1920. His father was a fruit inspector in that country, and Steve spent the first 10 years of his life there. But by 1930, both his father and mother had died. So Steve was sent to New Orleans to live with his grandmother.

In New Orleans, Steve saw his first football game. He decided then and there that he wanted to be a football player. When he was old enough, he tried out for the high school team, but he didn't make it. Steve weighed only 125 pounds, and the coach was afraid that he would get hurt playing the rough game of football.

Van Buren quit high school after only one year and took a job in an iron foundry. After two years of this hard work, he was heavier and stronger. When he went back to high school, Steve stood 6 feet tall and weighed 155 pounds. Now he was big enough for the team. Steve wanted to be a running back, but the coach made him play end. Unhappy about the coach's decision, Steve spent more time at another of his favorite sports—boxing.

Van Buren might have become a professional boxer after graduating from high school if he had not been offered a scholarship to Louisiana State University (LSU). He wanted an education even more than he wanted the money he could make boxing. So he accepted the scholarship. When he came to LSU in 1940, he tried out for football again. He still wanted to be a running back, but once again his hopes were crushed. The university already had a fine running back, Alvin Dark. Van Buren's job was to block for him.

Until his last year at LSU, all Steve did was block for Alvin Dark. But in 1943, Dark was called into the army. At last Van Buren was given a chance to run with the football. And he became an instant success. In six and a half games that season, he rushed for 847 yards in 150 carries, for a 5.6 yard average. When the season was over, he ranked second in the country in both rushing and scoring.

After just one year as a running back, Van Buren was drafted by the Philadelphia Eagles of the National Football League. By that time he was over 6 feet tall and weighed 200 pounds. He could run the 100-yard dash in 9.8 seconds. And Van Buren had power to match his speed. Instead of running past or around tacklers, he would often run right over them. In 1944, his first season with the Eagles, Steve played only four full games. Even so, he finished among the top five ball carriers in the NFL.

In 1945, Steve Van Buren saw his first full season as a running back, and the records began

*Steve Van Buren (Number 15) scores the only touchdown made during the 1948 NFL championship game.*

to fall. His 18 touchdowns that season set a new league mark. He averaged 5.8 yards each time he carried the ball.

The Flying Dutchman, as Van Buren was called, made the Eagles an NFL power. He brought them to their first Eastern Conference championship in 1947, and set a new rushing record of 1,008 yards. In 1948, he led his team to the NFL championship.

In 1949, Steve was the Eagles' star again. He rushed for a record 1,146 yards. (This record stood for nine years, until it was broken by the great Jim Brown of Cleveland.) It was in 1949 that the Philadelphia Eagles met the Los Angeles Rams for the NFL title. The game was played on a muddy field, and the Rams' great quarterback, Bob Waterfield, had trouble throwing the slippery ball. But the Eagles did not have to throw the ball at all. They let Van Buren run with it—31 times in all! Even though the Rams' defense was stacked to stop the Dutchman, he ran for 196 wet yards. The Eagles won the game—and their second NFL championship—14-0.

But trouble was about to strike. Just before the start of the 1950 season, Van Buren suffered a broken toe and a cracked rib. The toe was operated on, but it did not heal properly. Even with a pain-killing shot before each game, Steve could not run with the speed and power of his early years.

As the 1952 season began, his toe had at last started to heal. His ribs were in good shape, and Steve was ready to play his best. In the first practice game of the year, he took the ball and ran into the line. A first-year guard turned by mistake and hit Van Buren's knee from the side, injuring it badly. Steve Van Buren worked hard to come back from his injury, but he couldn't do it. He never carried the football in a game again.

After leaving pro football, Steve found it hard to make a new life for himself. But eventually, he was able to find a job coaching in a minor league. He also became a pro scout for the Eagles.

Today, experts look back on the Flying Dutchman's football career and try to see why he was so great. He did not have the ability to cut sharply while running. He did not have the size of some backs, or the speed of others. But he *was* a tough ball carrier who punished the defense. When he put his head down and ran, tacklers either moved out of the way or were knocked to the ground.

In 1965, Steve Van Buren, the player who was once too small to make the high school team, was elected to the Pro Football Hall of Fame.

# Joe Perry

Joe Perry is not as well known as most of the great pro running backs. This is partly because he never got the chance to play for a championship team. But people who study the game of football know about his outstanding abilities. When Joe came to the San Francisco 49ers in 1948, he set the pattern for a new kind of fullback. He did not have the size and power of other fullbacks, but he had fantastic speed.

Joe Perry was born in Arkansas in 1927, and grew up in Los Angeles. In high school he showed great promise in track and field. In track events, he was good in short dashes. And in field events he did well in the long jump, high jump, and shot put. But of all sporting events, football was Joe's favorite. Joe's mother did not want him to play this rough game, so he would sneak off to play without her knowing it. But his mother found out when an ankle injury swelled so large that he could not hide it. She decided that if he wanted to play football that badly, she would let him.

After graduating from high school in 1944, Joe enrolled at Compton Junior College and joined the football team. That first season, he scored 22 touchdowns for the team. Then he went into the navy. It was while he was playing for the Almeda, California, Naval Station team that he was first seen by professional scouts. The scouts saw him play in a game against San Francisco University. On that day, Joe Perry ran up and down the field like a wild bull. He had runs of 75, 85, 60, and 52 yards before he was taken out of the game for a rest.

Many professional teams wanted Joe to play for them, but he chose the San Francisco 49ers. Before he signed with the team, however, he wanted to run in the 1947 West Coast Relays, a contest of various track events. He entered the 100-yard dash at the relays even though he knew he had no chance of winning. He would have to run against the man who held the world record in the 100, Mel Patton. As it happened, Joe covered the distance in 9.5 seconds, just a step behind Patton.

In 1948, Perry reported to the 49ers training camp. He immediately made a place for himself at the fullback spot. In his rookie season he scored 10 touchdowns running, and averaged more than seven yards for each carry. But he did have a few problems. Like a sprinter, he always ran straight ahead. The 49ers worked at teaching him to use his speed to run around tacklers and not into them. After a while, he learned to do this. In his second season he rushed for 783 yards and was named all-conference fullback.

Joe Perry had found a place in football as a fullback. But as a black man, he had yet to find a place in the sport. At the same time that Joe was starting his pro football career, another famous black athlete, Jackie Robinson, was breaking the color barrier in baseball. Like Robinson, Joe Perry had to put up with mean words from both fans and players. Some of Joe's injuries on the field were caused by players who thought that he should not be playing in their league.

*Joe Perry (Number 34) breaks away from a Los Angeles tackler.*

But Joe *did* play in their league, and he became a star. In 1953, he became the only man in National Football League history to run for more than 1,000 yards in a season. And he won the rushing title again in 1954 with his best season total—1,049 yards.

Joe Perry played for the 49ers for 13 straight years. In 1952, he was joined in the 49er backfield by Hugh McElhenny, another great running back.

Together they gave San Francisco a tremendous running attack. But even with these two stars, the 49ers always seemed to lack the something that would make them champions.

In 1961, both men were traded, and Joe went to the Baltimore Colts. He thought about retiring, but football had become a way of life for him. The Colts needed a good running back, and Joe was their man. In his first game with Baltimore, he rushed for 108 yards in 18 carries to lead the Colts to win over Los Angeles. That season Joe was one of the NFL's top 10 rushers.

In 1962, Perry injured his knee in a pre-season game. It did not seem possible that the 35-year-old fullback could be well in time to play that year. But when the regular season started a month later, Joe was ready to play. He played well in 11 games, but he was not the Joe Perry of earlier days. The Colts let Perry go in 1963, and he went back to play his last year with the 49ers.

But the story does not end with Joe Perry's last year on the football field. For a few years he was a scout for the 49ers, and later an assistant coach. In 1969, Joe Perry was elected to the Pro Football Hall of Fame. His career had been a tough one in many ways. But in the end, he had won everyone's respect.

*Ollie Matson*

In 1959, the Los Angeles Rams were desperately trying to build a winning football team. To reach their goal, the Rams began trading for new players. The world of professional football was stunned when the Rams traded nine players to the Chicago Cardinals for one man. And that man was a 29-year-old running back whose best seasons were behind him. But that was how highly rated Ollie Matson was.

Ollie was born in Texas in 1930. He started playing football when he was very young. After his family moved to San Francisco, Matson played high school and college football there. During his one season on the San Francisco City College team, he ran for 19 touchdowns. He then enrolled at San Francisco University (SFU), a school with a very powerful football team. In 1951, with Matson at fullback, San Francisco went through its nine games without a loss. Ollie ran for 1,566 yards, which gave him a college total of 3,156 yards.

Once that season, San Francisco went to New York to play Fordham University. Before the game, the Eastern sportswriters were not impressed with Matson's or SFU's achievements. They were more impressed when Ollie ran for a 94-yard touchdown. Late in the game, the San Francisco team began to tire, and Fordham tied the score.

Matson himself was tired, but he took the kickoff and ran 90 yards for the last score of the game.

When he graduated from college, Ollie was drafted by the Chicago Cardinals of the National Football League. But before he played pro football, there was something else he wanted to do. Ollie knew that the Olympic Games were going to be held in 1952 at Helsinki, Finland. And what he wanted more than anything was to win a track medal in the Olympics. Distance running was his special skill.

To win a medal in track, Ollie knew he would have to be one of the first three finishers in his race, the 400-meter run. But football had changed his running style. He no longer had the long stride so important to a distance runner. Because of this, Ollie's chance of making the Olympic team didn't look good. But he worked hard to make his running style what it should be, and finally he made the U.S. Olympic team.

When Ollie Matson got to Finland, he did not win one medal—he won two. In the 400-meter race he ran against men who had trained years for that event. He took third place and a bronze medal. Later, he ran on the U.S. 1600-meter relay team, which won a gold (first-place) medal.

Ollie was back in Chicago in time to start the

1952 season with the Cardinals. In the second game, he revealed the skill that had led the Cardinals to draft him. He returned a kickoff 100 yards against the Bears for a score. During that season Ollie was a star on both offense and defense.

*Ollie Matson (Number 33) is hit by a tackler during a Cardinals-Steelers game in 1953.*

In 1954, after a year in the military service, Ollie returned to the Cardinals. But even with Ollie's help, the Cardinals' game did not improve.

The team was weak, especially when it came to blocking. Without good blocking, Matson had to fight all alone for many of the yards he gained. And he could seldom break through the line for a long run. In spite of the team's weakness, Ollie

*Playing for the Los Angeles Rams, Matson (right) tangles with the Vikings defense.*

was always ranked among the NFL's top rushers. And every year from 1954 to 1957, he was named to the NFL all-star team at the fullback spot.

Then came the famous trade in 1959, with Ollie going to the Los Angeles Rams in exchange for nine players. No one was surprised when the trade turned out bad for Los Angeles. The Rams had given away too many good players. But Matson did his part in that 1959 season. He gained 873 yards to rank third best in the NFL. In spite of Ollie's good work, however, the Rams got worse and worse. After the 1962 season the team traded Ollie to the Detroit Lions. Two years later he went to the Philadelphia Eagles, and there he found a home for a while. In 1964, he carried the football 96 times for 404 yards. He also returned kickoffs.

Ollie Matson retired from pro football in 1967. He had never played for a championship team, or even for a very good team. Because of this, he never got the publicity that other stars got. But fame or no fame, Ollie Matson ran for a total of 12,799 yards in his 14-year pro career. There is only one running back who did better—the great Jim Brown.

## Hugh McElhenny

When football people get together and talk about great open-field runners, one name always comes up in the conversation. That name is Hugh Mc-Elhenny. He was the greatest, the "King," of open-field runners. No one before Hugh McElhenny or after him has given the crowds the same electric thrill.

It is hard to believe there was a time when doctors thought that Hugh would never walk normally. As an 11-year-old kid in Los Angeles, Hugh stepped on a broken bottle, cutting all the tendons in his foot. Because of that injury, he missed a year of school. And he had to walk on crutches for seven months. But Hugh did special exercises, and soon his foot was almost as good as new.

There was another problem that almost kept Hugh from playing football—his father. Mr. McElhenny did not like football. He wanted his son to try out for the track team instead. As it happened, Hugh became a star in both track and football. In track, he ran the high and low hurdles and tied the world high-school record for the 120-yard high hurdles. The speed he developed in track events served him well in football. Hugh was not a big boy when he started playing football, but his speed made up for it. He could run the 100-yard dash in 9.7 seconds.

48

When McElhenny graduated from high school, he went to the University of Southern California, but he did not stay there long. He left the university and traveled across the country with a friend. Then he went back to California and enrolled at Compton Junior College. At Compton, he became a football star. Defensemen up and down the West Coast knew him as a runner to watch carefully. In his year at Compton, he led his team to the National Junior College Championship and scored 23 touchdowns.

After that year, Hugh's life changed. Several large universities had seen the kind of player he was. These universities wanted Hugh so badly that they even offered him money to play football for them. Hugh found it hard to turn down their offers. He finally decided to accept the offer of the University of Washington. (The school was later fined for breaking the recruiting rules.)

As long as Hugh played football, he had an easy life at Washington. With money almost rolling in, he was able to live a wild life. His style of football was wild too. In his three years at the U of W, Hugh set a Pacific Coast League record by gaining 2,499 yards. And in 1951, he was named to most of the All-America teams in the country.

In the 1952 pro football draft, McElhenny was

picked in the first round by the San Francisco 49ers. Life with the 49ers was quite a change for Hugh. In college he had been used to having a lot of money and fine things. So when he was drafted by the 49ers, he wanted $30,000 to sign with them. After the 49ers' owner explained to him that the NFL did not pay new players that much, Hugh finally agreed to sign for $7,000.

As a pro, Hugh McElhenny was an instant success. In his first season he rushed for 648 yards and six touchdowns. He led the NFL with a 7-yard average and was named to the all-star team. Hugh McElhenny had become the "King" of running backs. With his great combination of speed and balance, it was hard to knock him off his feet. When a tackler leaned one way to hit him, Hugh would cut the other way in a flash. Often the tackler would not even touch him.

The King played the 1954 season with a badly injured shoulder. The next year he injured his foot, but he played every game with the help of three pain-killing shots.

If 1954 and 1955 were tough years for Hugh, the next years were even worse for the 49ers.

*Hugh McElhenny (Number 39) scores a touchdown during a 49ers game against the Pittsburgh Steelers.*

With three other all-time greats in the backfield with Hugh—Y. A. Tittle, Joe Perry, and John Henry Johnson—the 49ers still could not win. The best they could do was to tie for the Western Conference championship in 1957. And they lost the playoff game to the Detroit Lions.

In 1961, the 49ers got rid of McElhenny, Perry, and Tittle. Hugh went to the Minnesota Vikings, a new team in the league. He was then past 30, with his best seasons behind him. But he helped build the Vikings into a strong team. With his open-field running, he was still a man to keep an eye on.

After two years with the Vikings, Hugh McElhenny was traded to the New York Giants. He helped the Giants to their 1963 NFL title, but he was traded again, in 1964, to the Detroit Lions. That was his last year in pro football, and he only played part time. But sometimes he would show the fans what the McElhenny of the mid-1950s was like. And when he showed them his speed and his style, everyone knew that he was still the King.

*Lenny Moore*

Lenny Moore was one of the most exciting of the great running backs of football. He had such speed and all-around ability that he was used as a pass receiver as often as a runner.

Lenny was born in Reading, Pennsylvania, in 1933, one of eight children of a poor family. As he grew, his natural skills began to show. At Reading High School his long legs made him a very good high jumper. His speed made him a star as an open-field runner on the football team. In fact, Lenny was such a good athlete that he did not have to practice hard at all. He could take it easy and still do well in games.

When Lenny left high school in 1952, many colleges offered him scholarships. But at last he chose to go to Penn State. As in high school, Lenny did not work hard in practice and did not take football seriously until Saturday afternoon. Then he exploded. He tore through defenses and dashed around tacklers on long runs. But all this was not enough to get him into professional football. He weighed only 175 pounds, and scouts were afraid that he might be hurt playing pro ball. The tacklers in professional football would be 50 to 100 pounds heavier than he.

Still, the Baltimore Colts were taking a long hard look at Lenny. They knew that he had gained almost eight yards for each carry in his last year at Penn State. The Colts liked what they saw and chose Lenny in the first round of the pro football draft. When Lenny came to training camp for the 1956 season, he was 15 pounds heavier and as fast as ever.

At that point, Moore had the ability to be a great pro player. But he did not have the right attitude. He still was not interested in working hard to develop his skills. Even so, in his rookie season, Lenny rushed for 649 yards for a 7.5-yard average. Many experts think he could have done even better.

Lenny's attitude about football finally changed because of a bad play in the 1957 season. The Colts were in the running for the National Football League championship that year. They had won their first three games and were close to beating the Detroit Lions in their fourth game. In trying to run out the clock, the Colts' star quarterback, Johnny Unitas, gave the ball to Lenny, and he fumbled. The Lions recovered the fumble and, seconds later, scored. After losing that game, Lenny made a promise to himself and to his team. He would work hard, very hard, in practice. He would develop his skills and try not to make mistakes.

Lenny followed through on his promise, and his

hard work paid off for both himself and the Colts. Baltimore won the NFL championship in both 1958 and 1959, and Moore was better than ever. If he was not thrilling the fans with his open-field running, he was catching long passes from Johnny Unitas.

Lenny Moore played a big part in the 1958 championship game, which is often called the greatest football game ever played. Playing against the New York Giants, Lenny showed the fans what a dangerous player could really do. The Giants were ahead, 17-14, with less than two minutes to play, when the Colts got the ball on their own 14-yard line. Time and again Moore ran deep, taking two or three defenders with him. At the same time, Unitas threw short passes that moved the Colts close enough for a game-tying field goal.

The two teams then went into pro football's first overtime period. The first team to score would win. For another 8 minutes Moore took the pass defenders with him, while Unitas threw to other receivers. Baltimore drove to a winning touchdown in 8 minutes and 15 seconds. The Colts had won the NFL title by a score of 23-17. A year later, they would win it again.

In 1960, Baltimore lost its NFL title to the Green Bay Packers. But Lenny Moore gained a title of his own. He was named all-conference halfback. Moore was really doing well. He was even being used by the Colts as a pass receiver. But then, in a pre-season game in 1962, Lenny was hurt. At the end of a 43-yard run, he fell out of bounds and cracked his knee cap. He missed the first six games of the season and did not play well in the remaining games. At the start of the next year, he had an

operation to take out his appendix. And later in the season he was kicked in the head and suffered dizzy spells for the rest of the year. Could even an athlete like Lenny Moore come back from such injuries?

In 1964 Moore left no doubt in the minds of those who were wondering. He shook off his problems and had his best season ever. He played and scored in every game, setting a season record by scoring 20 touchdowns. By then he had also become one of the best pass receivers in the league. He averaged more than 20 yards for each pass he caught. For his achievements that season, Lenny Moore was named the NFL's Most Valuable Player.

Lenny spent three more years with the Colts before retiring after the 1967 season. He had scored 113 touchdowns in his 12-year career, the second-best total in pro football history. Better than that, he had finally given his fans and teammates his best.

# Jim Brown

The football careers of many great running backs have been ended by injuries or by age. Only one was stopped by the movies—that of Jim Brown. Brown was still at the peak of his career in 1966 when he quit football to become a movie actor.

Brown was born on St. Simons Island, off the coast of Georgia, in 1936. Both his father and mother left home when he was very young, and he lived with his great-grandmother until he was seven. Then he went to live with his mother in New York City. As a boy, Jim joined a New York street gang called the Gaylords and became its leader. But his interest in high school athletics may have saved him from getting into real trouble. Jim had skills that helped him in every sport he played. He was a star in lacrosse, baseball, basketball, and track, as well as football.

When Jim graduated from high school, several colleges offered him scholarships to play football. It was a surprise to everyone when he chose Syracuse University, a school that would give him a scholarship only after he had proven himself. Even after he joined the Syracuse team, Jim found it hard to get the chance that he needed. At first he was the only black player on the team. And the coaches wanted him to play end instead of fullback. But in his second year Jim worked his way into the

starting backfield. Once there, he had no trouble proving himself. With Jim Brown running the ball, Syracuse became a national power. In his senior year there, he ran for 986 yards and was named to most of the All-America teams. And he was named an All-American in lacrosse as well.

But still, Jim was not thought of as the best professional football prospect in the country. Other players, like Paul Hornung and Jon Arnett, were picked in the pro draft before him. Brown was finally drafted by the Cleveland Browns, but he was their second choice. The Browns' first choice was Len Dawson, a quarterback who had been picked by another team.

Brown signed with the Cleveland Browns for $15,000 and went to his first pro training camp in 1957. At that time, Cleveland had a good fullback —Ed Modzelewski. Because the rookie Brown was trying to take Modzelewski's job, the veterans on the team took some hard shots at him. But those same players could not figure Brown out. No matter how hard they hit him, he never said a word on the field.

Ed Modzelewski did not resent Brown as the other players did. He saw what a fine player Jim could be, so he started helping the young rookie who would take his place. Jim did replace

Modzelewski during much of that first season in Cleveland. He was a success from the start, winning the NFL rushing title with 942 yards. In a game against the Los Angeles Rams, Brown set a one-game record of 237 yards in 31 carries.

In his first year, Jim Brown gave the Browns the lift they had needed. Cleveland had long been a power in pro football because of its great passing game. But the Browns' passing quarterback, Otto Graham, had retired. With Graham gone, the team did not look like a winner. But then came Jim Brown. Cleveland built a new offense around Brown's running and lost none of its offensive power.

But all was not still going well with the team. The Browns were winning games, but not championships. And Jim and the head coach, Paul Brown, were not getting along well. Jim described his problems with the coach during an interview before the Pro Bowl game in January 1962. In that interview Jim told a reporter that he was thinking of retiring.

He did not retire, but in 1962 he fell below the 1,000-yard mark in yards gained. He lost the rushing title, for the first and only time in his career, to Jim Taylor of Green Bay. Later it was found that the Cleveland fullback had played the

*Jim Brown is stopped by the New York Giants' Jim Patton.*

whole season with a badly injured wrist.

In 1962, the conflict between Jim and coach Brown grew worse. The conflict ended with the firing of Paul Brown by the Cleveland owner, Art Modell. Blanton Collier then became coach, and Jim Brown's running was given new life. Under coach Brown, Jim had been forced to follow the same plan every time a certain play was called. Collier let Jim run the way he thought best. If one hole closed up, Brown would run to find another hole in the line. Sometimes he might run around end. (In football, this is called "running to daylight.") This change in Brown's playing led to three of his best seasons. And he did more than just win rushing titles for those years. In 1963, he set an

NFL record of 1,863 yards gained. That record stood for 10 years before O. J. Simpson broke it in 1973.

Before the start of the 1965 season, Jim had been given a small part in a movie. He decided that he liked acting. Later, he got a bigger part in a war picture called *The Dirty Dozen.* The movie-making business began to take time from football, and it was clear that Jim had to choose between the two careers. Before the 1966 season began, Jim Brown retired from football.

When he retired, Jim took with him a string of records that will not soon be matched. But one record stands out above the rest. In his nine years with the Cleveland Browns, he rushed for a total of 12,312 yards. This is almost 4,000 yards more than the next man on the list. And Jim Brown quit before he was 30!

Many football experts say that Jim Brown was the greatest runner the game has ever known. He had straight-ahead driving power, but he was also fast and was able to change directions instantly. After being tackled, he always got up slowly and walked back to the huddle. Often he looked as if he did not have enough strength left to run another play. Then, on the next play, he would come back and hit the defense harder than before.

The story of Gale Sayers' football career is one of the most colorful and tragic stories of all of football history. No one knows how many records Sayers might have set if his career had not been cut short by injuries before he was 30. Even so, many football experts think that Gale was the best running back ever to play the game of football.

Gale Sayers was born on a farm in Kansas in 1943. Nine years later his family moved to Omaha, Nebraska, and it was there that Gale went to school. When he made the football team in high school, he wanted to be a linebacker. But that was no job for a player with Gale's speed. So the coach put him at halfback, where he could run with the ball. As it turned out, that was what Gale did best. He did it so well, in fact, that more than 100 colleges wanted him to play for their football teams.

Gale chose to go to the University of Kansas, a school that was not a college football power. Both

in college and later, during his professional career, Gale had the bad luck to play for weak teams. Because of this, the opposing team was always able to stack its defense to stop him. In spite of this problem, however, Gale won national fame at Kansas. His speed made him a dangerous man when he ran back punts and kickoffs. And running out of the backfield, Gale could break away for a long run at any time. In three years of college football he ran for a total of 2,675 yards, and a 6.5-yard average carry. The Kansas coach claimed that there was not even a pro running back who could outrun Gale.

During his college years, many people thought that Gale was almost without feelings. He never got excited, and the expression on his face never changed. But even though he was quiet, he did have very strong feelings about some things. Once while he was at Kansas, he was arrested for joining a protest over discrimination against blacks in student housing. Another time Gale spoke with feeling to a group of high school students in Chicago. He told them of the problem his father had because he had dropped out of school.

After college Gale was drafted by the Chicago Bears. When he went to their 1965 training camp, he met another young running back named Brian

Piccolo. Piccolo was white, and Sayers was black, and they were both trying for the same running-back spot. But still they became good friends. And they both became star running backs for the Bears—Sayers at halfback and Piccolo later at fullback. Then in 1969, cancer began to take away Piccolo's strength. When Brian Piccolo died in June 1970, Gale felt deep sadness. He wrote a story describing his and Brian's friendship, and the story was made into a popular movie, *Brian's Song*.

During his rookie year of 1965, Gale dazzled the National Football League with his ability. In one game he scored six touchdowns for 36 points. This was just four points less than the one-game record set by Ernie Nevers in 1929. Four of the touchdowns were on runs, one on a pass, and one on a punt return.

Also in the first season, he set an NFL record by scoring 22 touchdowns. And he rushed for over 800 yards, most of them gained on sweeps around end. Other teams began to set their defenses to stop these end runs. They thought that Sayers would not be able to run through the middle of the line as well as he had run around end.

They were wrong. In his second year with the Bears, Gale ran up the middle *and* around end. And he rolled up a total of 1,231 yards rushing to put him in the lead for the NFL rushing title. Going into the last game against the Minnesota Vikings—one of the toughest defensive teams in the league—Sayers needed 109 yards to win the rushing title. The Vikings knew that he was going to be getting the ball often. They stacked their defense to stop him, but Sayers ran through and around Viking tacklers for 197 yards.

*Gale Sayers (Number 40) runs with the ball during a game against the Green Bay Packers.*

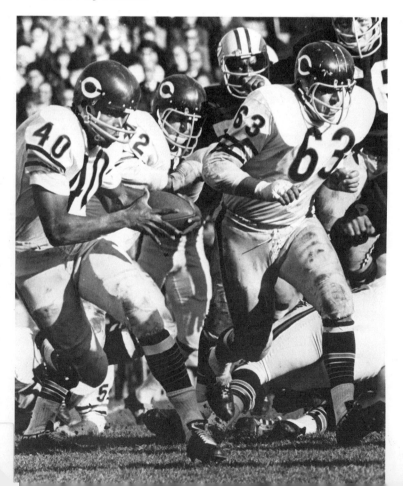

In 1968, his fourth season with the Bears, Gale was off to a great start. He almost tore apart a strong Green Bay team, running for 205 yards in 24 carries. Before the San Francisco 49er game, he had more than 800 yards rushing. It seemed that he would surely finish the season with more than 1,000. But during that game, a 49er hit him around the knees, injuring him badly. Gale was carried from the field and was operated on that same day.

After his injury Gale played again, but not for long. He never quite regained the form of his early years. Gale finally was forced into retirement in 1971. He was only 28, an age at which most players are just reaching the high point of their careers.

People who know football often think of Gale Sayers as a new kind of running back. He had the speed and shiftiness of a halfback and the power of a fullback. And once he got into the open field, few people could touch him. One NFL player put it this way. "He doesn't look any different than any other back coming at you. But when he gets there, he's *gone*."

# *About the Author*

Richard Rainbolt is a longtime sports fan who has written a number of lively, well-received sports books. Among them are *Gold Glory*, a history of the Minnesota Gophers; *The Goldy Shuffle*, the story of Bill Goldsworthy of the Minnesota North Stars; and *The Minnesota Vikings*, a fast-paced history of that famous team. As one might guess from his books, the author is a native of Minnesota. After serving in the U.S. Marines, Mr. Rainbolt attended the University of Minnesota, where he received a degree in journalism. Since then, he has worked as a newspaper reporter, a public relations man, and a reporter for the Associated Press. In addition to writing, Mr. Rainbolt now runs his own public relations firm.

10,101

920
Ra        Rainbolt, Richard
             Football's rugged
          running backs.

| MAR 23 1982 | DATE DUE | | |
|---|---|---|---|
| APR 2 1982 | JAN 2 0 1984 | FEB 14 '85 | |
| OCT 1 1982 | APR 5 1984 | | |
| NOV 4 1983 | SEP 2 0 1984 | | |
| MAY 18 1983 | OCT 1 1984 | MAR 24 '86 | |
| NOV 3 1983 | FEB 14 '85 | OCT 16 1987 | |
| NOV 2 9 1983 | APR 10 '86 | DEC 2 1987 | |
| DEC 8 1983 | FEB 19 '86 | DEC 22 1987 | |
| JAN 4 1984 | APR 7 1987 | | |
| | OCT 16 1987 | | |
| MAR 23 1984 | OCT 22 1987 | | |
| JAN 4 1985 | | | |